LON

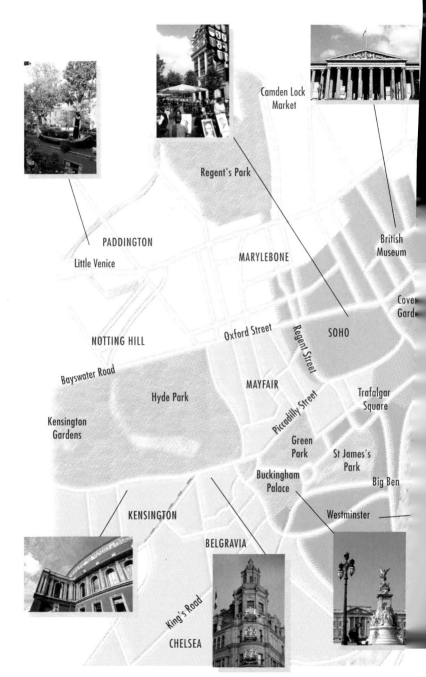

Camden Lock Market

Regent's Park

British Museum

PADDINGTON

Little Venice

MARYLEBONE

Cove Gard

NOTTING HILL

Oxford Street

Regent Street

SOHO

Bayswater Road

MAYFAIR

Hyde Park

Piccadilly Street

Trafalgar Square

Kensington Gardens

Green Park

St James's Park

Buckingham Palace

Big Ben

KENSINGTON

Westminster

BELGRAVIA

King's Road

CHELSEA

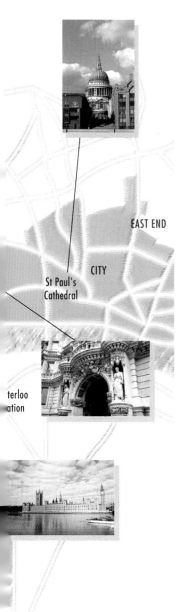

EAST END

CITY

St Paul's
Cathedral

terloo
ation

This clock tower stands 348 feet (106 m) tall and houses the largest clock in Britain as well as Big Ben, the world-famous bell, which weighs over 13 tonnes.

I n the historical heart of the City, St Paul's Cathedral and the Tower of London rub shoulders with the London Stock Exchange.

CITY OF LONDON

The dragon is the symbol of the City.

The City of London

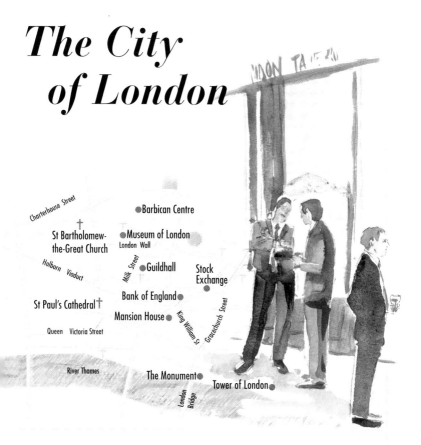

Charterhouse Street

St Bartholomew-the-Great Church

●Barbican Centre

●Museum of London
London Wall

Holborn Viaduct

Milk Street ●Guildhall

Stock Exchange

St Paul's Cathedral †

Bank of England●

Mansion House ●

King William St

Gracechurch Street

Queen Victoria Street

River Thames

The Monument●

Tower of London●

London Bridge

The Palace of Westminster has been rebuilt several times. The present building is Gothic Revival in style and dates from the middle of the 19th century.

The Thames has always played a crucial part in London's economic growth.

From Londinium to London

Londinium, built by the Romans some 2000 years ago, was destined to become an important centre of trade and its strategic position on the banks of the Thames ensured

London is a city in which the old rubs shoulders with the new. The famous London taxi cabs – traditionally made by Austin – were once all black. Whilst this is still largely true today, many now sport brightly coloured advertisements on their bodywork.

that London would continue to expand over the following centuries.

7

The Guildhall serves as the town hall of the City of London.

In 60 AD, the Roman historian Publius Tacitus described Londinium, the former name of London, as a booming centre of trade. Since then, the city has continued to develop, going from strength to strength. In the Middle Ages, members of trade

The Church of St Mary-le-Bow is famous for its bells, known as the Bow Bells. Cockneys, the inhabitants of London's East End, are only worthy of the name if they were born within earshot of the bells.

guilds built the **Guildhall** which served as both a meeting place for merchants, who controlled the city's wealth, and the administrative offices of the city.

The architect Nicholas Hawks-moor (1661–1736), a student of Christopher Wren, designed the Church of St Mary Woolnoth in the English baroque style, using a much freer interpretation than his predecessors.

As time went by, London's commercial centre became increasingly independent of the Crown. In 1215, King John defined its privileges and autonomy in the Magna Carta. In 1666, the Great Fire of London almost completely destroyed the City of London. Christopher Wren (1632–1723) was put in charge of rebuilding 52 of the City's churches, including St Paul's Cathedral and the Church of **St Mary-le-Bow** (completed in 1680). Like many other of the City's churches, the latter was largely destroyed by bombs during World War II and has since been restored.

The break with the Papacy

The break with the Roman Catholic Church began in the 16th century, during the reign of Henry VIII, when the Pope refused to grant the king a divorce from his first wife, Catherine of Aragon. Henry went on to marry five more times, with marriages to Anne Boleyn, Jane Seymour, Anne of Cleves, Catherine Howard and Catherine Parr, and in 1534, decided to break completely with Rome. Despite many diplomatic and religious complications, he founded the Church of England. As a result of this, ownership of Church property passed to the English Crown. Conversely, the monarchy became responsible for the funding of hospitals and provision of education, which until then had been the preserve of monasteries.

The Bank of England, known as the 'Old Lady of Threadneedle Street'.

The Church of St Mary Abchurch, started in 1681, is widely regarded as the most elegant of those built by Wren. As Surveyor of the King's Works, Wren built St Paul's Cathedral and designed more than 50 other churches over a period of more than 30 years. His unique architectural style is one that combines baroque, Renaissance and classical elements.

The **Bank of England** was established in 1694 to finance the war against France and still dominates Britain's money markets today. Close by stands **Mansion House** (1753), the official residence of the Lord Mayor of London. The building symbolizes both the Lord Mayor's and the City's independence of the sovereign.

The Corinthian columns of Mansion House.

Many pubs in the City are hidden away down alleyways, far from the hustle and bustle of the capital's streets and tourist attractions.

More than 350,000 people work at the Stock Exchange and in the financial markets. The dress code is now more relaxed, and whilst the sober suit remains, the black bowler hat and umbrella, once the uniform of the City Gent, are largely a thing of the past.

Back in 1192, London's merchants elected a representative, the mayor (who later became known as the Lord Mayor). To this day, the City of London remains an independent entity with its own administration. On the day of her coronation in 1953, before entering the City, Queen Elizabeth II had to declare that she was coming with peaceful intentions.

Lunchtime in the City: The frantic activity that characterizes this area of London during the week dies down at the weekend and a contrasting atmosphere of quiet and calm descends on the streets. Only 6000 people actually live in the financial heart of London.

The famous red double-decker buses remain the cheapest way of getting around London.

The Lloyd's Building, built in 1986.

The traditional London black cab, designed by Austin in 1959, now comes in other colours.
Cab drivers are all tested on their knowledge of London before being granted a licence and will thus be able to find the quickest route to your destination.

Despite being bombed during the winter of 1940–41, the 'Square Mile', an alternative name for the City of London which covers just 1 square mile (2.6 square kilometres), displays a rich variety of architectural styles. Futuristic high-rise towers, like the **Lloyd's Building**, stand alongside neoclassical Victorian buildings, such as the **Royal Exchange**.

This stone column, known simply as the Monument, is over 200 feet (60 m) tall.

The **Monument** is the tallest Doric column in the world. It was erected to commemorate the rebuilding of London after the Great Fire of September 1666. Its height equals the distance between its base and the baker's shop in Pudding Lane where the fire started. Take the 311 steps to the top for a panoramic view of the City.

The City is now almost entirely taken up by buildings devoted to the powerful financial markets whilst the large food markets of the past have now closed down.

As a result, Leadenhall Market is now full of specialist food shops and small eateries. This elegant hall, with its majestic dome and rich decor, was designed in 1881 by the architect Sir Horace Jones.

The dome of St Paul's Cathedral, rising above the great central nave, is decorated with monochrome frescoes by James Thornhill illustrating scenes from the life of St Paul.

The pediment on the top of St Paul's Cathedral was carved in 1706.

St Paul's Cathedral

Standing at the heart of medieval London, St Paul's Cathedral has dominated the city as a religious and historical landmark for centuries. Today, it is also home to St Paul's Choir, one of the country's most prestigious cathedral choirs.

The great dome that tops St Paul's Cathedral takes the overall height to 365 feet (110 m), one foot for each day of the year. Rising to a height of 111 feet (34 m), the dome is the second-largest in the world, surpassed only by St Peter's in Rome.

The ornate decoration enhances the nave of St Paul's Cathedral.

Having decided to renovate the existing **St Paul's Cathedral**, the authorities approved a design by Wren on August 27, 1666. Just one week later, however, the building, the largest in the Western Christian world, was destroyed by

This statue of Queen Anne, dating from 1886, stands in the square in front of St Paul's Cathedral.

The nave, 450 feet (152 metres) long, is one of the building's most impressive features.

the Great Fire. Wren, appointed Surveyor of the King's Works, was then charged with the complete rebuilding of the cathedral which was to take more than 30 years to complete.

The tomb of Sir Christopher Wren is marked by an inscription in the floor of the cathedral. It reads: 'Lector, si monumentum requiris, circumspice' ('Reader, if you seek his monument, look around you').

Choristers and whispers

The choir of St Paul's Cathedral is one of the most prestigious cathedral choirs in Britain, performing both at royal ceremonies and for the general public. Those with an interest in choral music should head for the cathedral at around 5 pm where the choir sings at evensong every day.

Younger visitors to the cathedral will enjoy sharing secrets in the famous Whispering Gallery which runs round the interior of the dome, 30 metres above the ground. Thanks to a peculiar acoustic effect, the quietest whisper can be clearly heard from one side of the gallery to the other.

The dome, rising to a height of 365 feet (110 metres), displays an original combination of baroque and Italian Renaissance styles. In the crypt lie the tombs of many famous people, as well as memorials to Sir Winston Churchill and Lawrence of Arabia. The nave, meanwhile, is decorated with paintings by major 18th-century artists. These hallowed walls have witnessed some of the country's most important royal ceremonies, such as the Golden Jubilee of Queen Victoria in 1887 and the wedding of Prince Charles and Lady Diana Spencer in 1981.

The Museum of London, which faces the Old London Wall, a Roman rampart dating from the 3rd century, traces the entire history of the capital through reconstructed street scenes, working models and a wealth of objects from various periods.

Nearby is the Barbican Centre which was opened in 1982. It contains two theatres, cinemas and an art gallery and is also home to the Royal Shakespeare Company and the world-famous London Symphony Orchestra.

In Smithfield, not far from the Church of St Bartholomew-the-Great, stands St Bartholomew's Hospital. This is the oldest hospital in London, founded in 1123, although the oldest surviving buildings date from 1759.

The porch of St Bartholomew-the-Great.

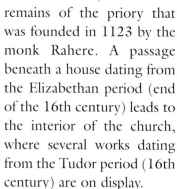

St Bartholomew-the-Great, one of the oldest churches in London, is all that remains of the priory that was founded in 1123 by the monk Rahere. A passage beneath a house dating from the Elizabethan period (end of the 16th century) leads to the interior of the church, where several works dating from the Tudor period (16th century) are on display.

Charterhouse Square, with its gas lamps, contains vestiges of a medieval monastery founded in the 4th century and inhabited by Carthusian monks.

This military stronghold was built by William the Conqueror and enlarged by succeeding monarchs. In its final form, the Tower of London numbers 22 towers.

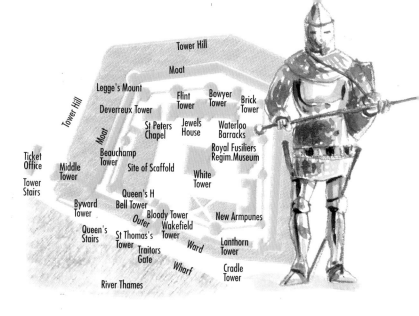

Tower Hill

Moat

Legge's Mount

Flint Tower
Bowyer Tower
Brick Tower

Tower Hill

Deverreux Tower

St Peters Chapel
Jewels House
Waterloo Barracks

Moat

Royal Fusiliers Regim.Museum

Ticket Office

Beauchamp Tower

Middle Tower

Site of Scaffold

White Tower

Tower Stairs

Queen's H

Byward Tower
Bell Tower

Outer

Bloody Tower

Queen's Stairs
St Thomas's Tower

Wakefield Tower

New Armpunes

Traitors Gate

Ward

Lanthorn Tower

Wharf

Cradle Tower

River Thames

The Tower of London and Tower Bridge

The Tower of London, once a royal residence and state prison, is today one of London's largest tourist attractions. Along with Tower Bridge, it emphasizes

Every evening, at 9.53 pm, the keys of the Tower are handed over to the Governor, a representative of the Queen who resides at the Tower. The ceremony itself lasts just seven minutes, ending as the Tower clock strikes ten.

the important role played by the Thames during the history of the city.

The Yeoman Warders, also referred to as Beefeaters, guard the fortress and take part in the ceremonial handing over of the keys. They are also in charge of the famous royal ravens. These birds have their wings clipped since, according to legend, if they leave the Tower, it will collapse, bringing down the entire kingdom with it.

One of the 22 stone towers.

The Tower of London is surrounded by a moat and curtain wall. The moat, 130 feet (40 m) deep, is now dry. A bowling green and tennis court have been opened there for use by the 150 residents of the Tower, including the famous Yeoman Warders.

Crowned King of England on Christmas Day 1066, William the Conqueror ordered fortifications to be raised to protect London. The **Tower of London** was built on the banks of the Thames to ward off possible attack from invaders approaching from the sea. The fortress that was reputedly impregnable today houses the **Crown Jewels**. Among these are the solid

The White Tower takes its name from the light-coloured stone used to build it.

gold St Edward's crown, used at the coronation of Charles II in 1661, the Imperial Crown of India, set with over 6000 diamonds, the Queen Mother's Crown (1937), containing the Koh-i-noor Diamond, the hollow gold orb and the royal sceptre on which is set the First Star of Africa, the largest cut diamond in the world.

The Tower of London was once used as a royal residence. In the 16th century, however, during the reign of Henry VIII, it became the main state prison in which more than one of his wives spent time. Anne Boleyn, his second wife, was held there before being beheaded in 1536, to be followed by Catherine Howard, his fifth wife, who was executed in 1542.

Tower Bridge's two towers consist of a steel skeleton clad in neo-Gothic stonework.

Since 1982, a museum in one of the towers of Tower Bridge has explained the history of the bridge. Exhibits include preliminary plans by the bridge's architect, Sir Horace Jones, and drawings by Stevenson, who made changes to its structure.

Among the great engineering projects of the British Empire, created at the dawn of the Industrial Revolution, is **Tower Bridge**, a symbol of the capital and feat of architectural and technical prowess. Spanning 2640 feet (805 metres), the bridge incorporates two bascules, 30 feet (9 metres) above water level, which swing open so that large vessels can pass under the bridge. Up until 1976, the bascules were raised by a

Tower Bridge offers a view of the different architectural styles of London.

steam-driven mechanism. This operation, which took under 2 minutes, was regularly carried out up to five times a day when river traffic was busy. Today, however, the bascules, each of which weighs 1100 tonnes, are raised only on exceptional occasions. The pedestrian footway was closed in 1911 because of the large number of suicides that took place there. It is now enclosed in glass and can be reached either by taking one of the lifts or by climbing the 300 stairs. The view from the footway over the Tower of London and the Thames is truly spectacular.

Tower Bridge's two neo-Gothic towers house the hydraulic mechanism that raises the bascules in under two minutes. In 1976, the steam mechanism that carried out this operation was replaced by a hydroelectric system.

Anchored upstream from Tower Bridge since 1971, the ex-Royal Navy cruiser HMS Belfast was used during World War II and is now a floating naval museum.

The room containing the lifting mechanism is now open to the public.

Tower Bridge was opened in 1894.

As it flows through the centre of the capital, the River Thames is spanned by eleven bridges. The first was London Bridge, built in 1209 and lined at that time with buildings. Many of these were destroyed in the Great Fire of London (1666). The current London Bridge dates from 1971.

The steel skeleton sheathed in stone is today universally admired. When it was opened, however, it was the object of fierce public criticism. At that time, opinion was deeply divided on the pros and cons of covering the metal structure in stone. For all this disagreement, the bridge stands today as a monument to the sheer extravagance of the age.

The neo-Gothic style of Tower Bridge was imposed by the City of London and Parliament. This heavy stonework also ensures a more stable roadway.

Victoria Tower, 336 feet (104 m) high, forms part of the Houses of Parliament. Here, over 3 million parliamentary documents are stored.

While the seat of financial power is the City, royal, religious and political power is still centred around Westminster.

Horse Guards Parade.

The seat of power

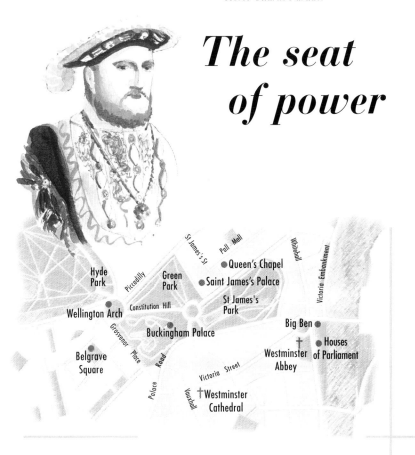

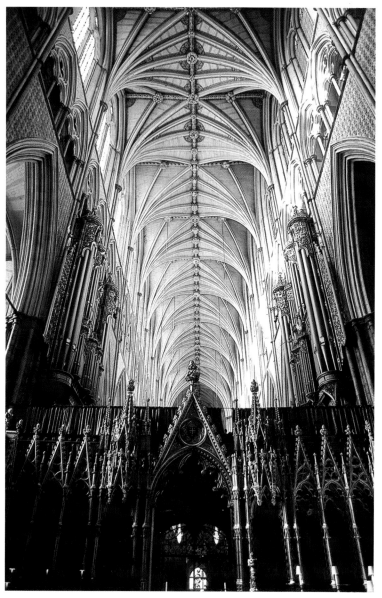

Some 32 feet (10 m) wide and 100 feet (31 m) high, the nave of Westminster Abbey appears surprisingly narrow and gives the impression of soaring skywards.

The choir stalls in Westminster Abbey.

Westminster

Westminster Abbey has strong royal connections, serving as the stage for the weddings, funerals and coronations of kings and queens. It stands opposite the

After the canonization of Edward the Confessor (c. 1003–1066), who was responsible for restoring the Anglo-Saxon monarchy to England, Westminster Abbey became the focus of pilgrimage. Within its walls, most of the kings and queens of England have been crowned.

Palace of Westminster which is today the seat of the British parliament.

Fan vaulting adorns the ceiling of the Lady Chapel within Westminster Abbey.

Given that it has been altered many times in the course of its history, **Westminster Abbey** presents a mixture of styles. The present-day building dates from 1245 and although many additions were made over the following centuries,

Above: Dean's Yard, adjacent to Westminster Abbey, is used by the pupils of Westminster School.
Left: This Statue of Shakespeare is in Poets' Corner in the Abbey.

the result is a harmonious mixture of the earliest Gothic architecture that is French in inspiration, and the Flamboyant style that is typical of later English Gothic.

The entrance to Westminster Abbey is at the west side of the building. The two towers, built by Sir Nicholas Hawksmoor in the middle of the 18th century, show a certain French influence, inspired by the cathedral at Rheims.

Poets' Corner

No trip to Westminster Abbey would be complete without a visit to Poets' Corner, which lies off the south transept. Memorials to William Shakespeare (1564–1616), John Milton (1608–1674) and John Keats (1795–1821) are but three of the many monuments that stand in memory of the greatest figures in English literature. Such illustrious names must surely inspire the pupils of Westminster School as they stroll out into Dean's Yard, the square that joins onto this prestigious school, to read or relax, just as the poet John Dryden (1631–1700) and the playwright Ben Jonson (1572–1637) would have done in their day.

Two of the abbey's chapels are of particular interest. The Henry VII Chapel houses many royal tombs, including those of Henry VII and Elizabeth of York, Mary Tudor and Elizabeth I. In St Edward's Chapel lies the tomb of Edward the Confessor, who founded the original abbey in 1050. Close by stands the ancient oak Coronation Chair which until recently stood over the Stone of Scone. Seized from the Scots by Edward the Confessor in 1297, the stone remained at Westminster Abbey until 1996, when it was returned to Scotland.

The clock tower of the Houses of Parliament contains Big Ben, the famous bell which sounded for the first time on May 31, 1859.

The Houses of the Parliament symbolize Britain's parliamentary monarchy.

The **Houses of Parliament** are a true masterpiece of architecture in the Victorian Gothic Revival style. They were built by the architect Sir Charles Barry and stand on the site of a medieval royal residence, the Palace of Westminster, which served as the seat of Parliament from 1512 until it was destroyed by fire in 1834.

After the death of Sir Charles Barry (1795–1860), his son, Edward, continued work on the new Palace of Westminster. This statue of Oliver Cromwell stands in front of Westminster Hall where many trials and historical events have taken place. It was here that Edward II delivered his resignation speech in 1327 and that Charles I was condemned to death in 1649.

Big Ben is generally thought to be named after Benjamin Hall who was head of public works in the middle of the 19th century.

The equestrian statue of Richard the Lion-heart was made by Carlo Marochetti in 1860.

On November 5, 1605, during the State Opening of Parliament in the presence of King James I, Guy Fawkes was arrested as he prepared to blow up the building. Ever since, the cellars beneath the Houses of Parliament are searched at the annual State Opening of Parliament.

A fine example of the Gothic Revival style.

In Britain, legislative power is shared between the **House of Lords**, made up of peers of the land, and the **House of Commons**, made up of elected Members of Parliament (or MPs).

Since 1859, the business of the two houses has been punctuated by the chimes of **Big Ben**, the name of the bell in the clock tower which strikes the hour.

The majestic Palace of Westminster, seat of the British parliament.

Until 1882, **Westminster Hall** (1097), the only vestige of the original palace, housed the main tribunals and courts of justice. The head of Oliver Cromwell, who died in 1658, was put on display on the roof of the hall, where it remained for over 20 years. Today, this building serves as the lobby of the House of Commons.

The statue of Boudicca, the Queen of the Iceni who fought with Roman invaders in 60 AD, stands at the entrance to Westminster Bridge.

The ceremony of Changing of the Guard is exactly the same as it was when it was first introduced in 1660, when regiments were appointed to protect the monarch. The ceremony itself starts from Parliament Street.

The rear façade of Whitehall Palace.

The Royal Horse Guards, the Queen's own cavalry regiment, are changed twice a day. The Blues and Royals are identifiable by their blue tunics and the red plumes in their helmets.

The British government's most important ministries and main departments are concentrated in **Whitehall**, an area located between Westminster and Charing Cross. The name Whitehall refers to the old palace that was destroyed by fire in 1698. Of this only the **Banqueting House** survives, noted for the paintings by Peter Paul Rubens that decorate its great ceiling. This vast decorative scheme, commissioned by Charles I in 1630, glorifies the reign of James I (1566–1625). On the wide esplanade known as Horse Guards Parade, the Queen's official birthday is marked by

A sentry on horseback at the entrance to Horse Guards Parade.

Trooping the Colour, a military ceremony in which the regimental guards present their flag to the monarch. Nearby stands **Downing Street**, a narrow street in which, at No. 10, nestles the Prime Minister's residence. At the end of King Charles Street are the **Cabinet War Rooms**, the underground chambers that were the centre of British government and its military headquarters during World War II.

Certain areas of the Cabinet War Rooms were used by Sir Winston Churchill during World War II.

The official residence of the British Prime Minister is at 10 Downing Street. Next door at number 11, lives the Chancellor of the Exchequer.

Fashions may come and go but traditional dress is still de rigueur at important social events, such as Royal Ascot.

Prince Charles was invested Prince of Wales in 1969.

Royal London

With its palaces, parks and majestic Mall, royal London attracts millions of visitors from all over the world. In this aristocratic setting, royal traditions and

The inscription 'E II R' (Elizabeth II Regina) is a symbol of the current British monarchy. The Queen was born in London in 1926. She married Prince Philip of Greece, the Duke of Edinburgh, in 1947 and acceded to the throne in February 1952.

ceremonies have gone unchanged for many hundreds of years.

Admiralty Arch (1911) was erected in memory of Queen Victoria who died in 1901.

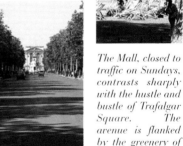

Admiralty Arch marks the entrance to the royal city. Designed by Sir Aston Webb at the beginning of the 20th century, it separates royal London from the lively area of Trafalgar Square. During royal ceremonies or processions, the gate in

The Mall, closed to traffic on Sundays, contrasts sharply with the hustle and bustle of Trafalgar Square. The avenue is flanked by the greenery of St James's Park and its lake.

the central arch is opened onto the **Mall** which leads up to Buckingham Palace. This avenue, transformed by Webb in 1911, then becomes the focus of public attention.

Royal Power

From the bridge that spans the lake in St James's Park, Buckingham Palace can be seen clearly in the distance.

For many British people, the monarchy remains the cornerstone of the State. Whether affected by the solemnity of sad events or buoyed up by grand State occasions, they readily express their attachment to the Crown, under which are united the four realms of the United Kingdom (England, Scotland and Wales, which constitute Great Britain, and Northern Ireland). Even though the Queen has no executive power, she approves the election of the Prime Minister and has the power to dissolve Parliament. She presides over many official ceremonies, most of which go back to the Middle Ages. She is also head of the Anglican Church and the Commonwealth.

On the southern side of the Mall, from Admiralty Arch up to Buckingham Palace, lies **St James's Park**, the smallest but also the oldest of London's royal parks. In 1532, this former area of marshland was drained and used as a hunting ground by Henry VIII. Today it is a haven for the many species of birds that have made their home in London, most notably the royal swans, which belong to the Queen. At lunchtime, local office workers come to the park to relax in one of the many deck chairs that are laid out on the grass alongside picnickers and sunbathers.

The fortified entrance to St James's Palace, defended by the Royal Guard.

The Changing of the Guard lasts for about 40 minutes. The old and new guards meet at 11.30 am in the forecourt of Buckingham Palace and, to the sound of trumpets and drums, the keys of the palace are handed over.

St James's Palace, built by Henry VIII in 1532, stands on the site of an old leper hospital. This Tudor-style palace became a permanent royal residence after the fire of 1698 that destroyed Whitehall, and remained so until the accession of Queen Victoria who, in 1837, decided to move home to Buckingham Palace. As a legacy from that time, the English court is still known as 'the Court of St James'.

Buttons and decorations on the uniform of a Life Guard.

St James's Palace, with its distinctive octagonal towers, is now home to the Lord Chamberlain and certain members of the Queen's Household. Separated from the palace by Marlborough Gate is the **Queen's Chapel**. This chapel was built by Inigo Jones and is the first building in England to be designed in the classical style. Inside is a magnificent altarpiece by Annibale Carracci. This, the Queen's private chapel, is unfortunately normally closed to the public and is open only during Sunday morning services between Easter and the end of July.

The five British infantry regiments (the Grenadier Guards, the Coldstream Guards, the Scots Guards, the Irish Guards and the Welsh Guards) can be told apart by their buttons and the colour of the feather in their bearskins.

The Queen Victoria Memorial stands in front of Buckingham Palace. The royal standard only flies over the palace when the Queen is in residence.

The Royal Guards stand to attention in front of Buckingham Palace.

Buckingham Palace, a royal residence since 1837, was built by the architect John Nash who converted the original Buckingham House into a palace during the reign of George IV. Certain state apartments are open to the public in July and August. On certain special occasions, the Royal Family appears on the balcony that faces the Mall. In the **Queen's Gallery**, paintings forming part of the Royal Collection are displayed.

The royal motto 'Dieu et mon droit' dates back to the time of Richard the Lionheart, when French was the official language at the English court.

The lion and the unicorn on the royal coat of arms symbolize the Crown's rule over Scotland.

Hyde Park, not far from Buckingham Palace, is an ideal place for horse riding.

A suitably large and impressive building was needed for the Great Exhibition of 1851. Joseph Paxton's Crystal Palace was the winning design. This great iron and glass hall was erected in Hyde Park using 4500 tonnes of iron and 400 tonnes of glass. It was later transferred to south London, where it was used as a leisure centre before being destroyed by fire in 1936.

Hyde Park, which covers 615 acres (249 hectares), is London's largest park. The Great Exhibition of 1851 was held there in the famous **Crystal Palace**, now no longer standing. **Rotten Row**, which cuts through the park, was the first public highway in England to be lit: 300 lanterns were suspended from the trees that lined the

Deck chairs for hire in Hyde Park.

Marble Arch was originally the entrance to Buckingham Palace but was too narrow for the royal coaches. It was transferred to the north-eastern corner of Hyde Park in 1851.

The Christmas Day swim in the Serpentine is a tradition that lives on. When it is frozen, intrepid swimmers think nothing of breaking the ice!

route to discourage muggers. The **Serpentine**, an artificial lake, was made in 1730 for Queen Caroline, a keen landscape gardener. Today, there are rowing boats for hire and one section is open for public swimming. At **Speakers' Corner**, next to Marble Arch, a law passed in 1872 allows anyone to publicly air their views on any subject.

Whilst it is horse racing that is traditionally known as 'the sport of kings', at least one member of the royal family, Prince Charles, is also a keen polo player. Originally from Central Asia, polo was brought to England from India in the late 19th century.

49

Kensington Palace seen from Kensington Gardens.

The eastern side of Hyde Park merges neatly into **Kensington Gardens**. Designed by Queen Caroline, these were once the private gardens of Kensington Palace but have been open to the public since 1841 and are home to various statues,

Queen Victoria was born in Kensington Palace in 1819. Some rooms are open to the public and there is a permanent exhibition of court attire spanning two centuries.

including the **Albert Memorial**. A favourite with children is the statue of Peter Pan (made in 1912), the well-known character created by the author J.M. Barry in 1904.

The Round Pond in Kensington Gardens is enjoyed by young and old alike, especially those who like to sail their model boats.

On New Year's Eve, Londoners traditionally gather around the fountains in Trafalgar Square to see in the New Year.

O n the banks of the Thames, b e t w e e n theatreland and the more austere realm of lawyers, London has many treasures to offer.

The Red Lion, one of London's pubs.

Trafalgar Square to Temple

From the top of Nelson's Column, 184 feet (56 metres) high, the statue of Lord Nelson surveys Trafalgar Square, the focal point of all kinds of rallies and demonstrations.

The National Gallery holds the finest collection of Italian painting outside Italy.

Trafalgar Square

This lively area, which stretches as far as Charing Cross, the official geographical centre of London, is famous for both its memorial to the days when England was a great naval power and the art collections of the National Gallery.

The National Portrait Gallery traces the art of British portraiture from the 14th century to the present day. On display are portraits ranging from King Henry VIII and Shakespeare to Margaret Thatcher and Mick Jagger.

The National Gallery stands on the northern side of Trafalgar Square.

During World War II, Great Britain offered protection to the exiled royal family of Norway. Ever since 1947, the city of Oslo has sent an enormous Christmas tree to London as a gift of thanks. The tree is set up in **Trafalgar Square**

Left: Nelson's Column (1842) commemorates the famous British admiral who died at the Battle of Trafalgar in 1805.

which is also the main venue for many public celebrations. On the night of December 31, crowds gather around Nelson's Column to welcome in the New Year.

The four lions that lie at the foot of Nelson's Column have guarded the monument since 1867. They are the work of E d w a r d Landseer, the animal painter and court artist.

The **National Gallery**, on the north side of Trafalgar Square, contains some 2000 paintings. It was established in 1824 after the British government had acquired 38 Old Master paintings, including works by Rembrandt, Rubens, Raphael and Titian. Today this national collection also includes such masterpieces as the *Arnolfini Marriage* by Jan van Eyck, *The Rout of San Romano* by Paolo Uccello, *The Ambassadors* by Hans Holbein, *Rokeby Venus* by Diego Velasquez, *Les Grandes Baigneuses* by Paul Cézanne and *Bathers at Asnières* by Georges Seurat.

Lord Nelson

Having joined the navy at the age of 12, Horatio Nelson became a lieutenant at 19 and a naval captain at 21, losing his right eye at the siege of Calvi. For the part that he played in the victory secured off Cape St Vincent, in Portugal, he was rewarded with the title of Rear Admiral and made a Companion of the Order of the Bath. But it was the three naval victories – the Battle of the Nile in 1798, the Battle of Copenhagen in 1800 and the Battle of Trafalgar in 1805, where he was killed – that made him a hero in British eyes. These victories ensured that England retained command of the seas. Nelson's dying words 'Thank God I have done my duty' have passed into legend.

The National Portrait Gallery nestles on the eastern side of the National Gallery.

The collection of paintings at the National Gallery spans almost five centuries. The building consists of four wings in which the various collections are displayed in chronological sections. Some 2000 paintings, by artists ranging from Botticelli to Picasso, make this one of the most impressive art galleries in the world.

The Church of **St-Martin-in-the-Fields**, completed in 1726, is the oldest building in Trafalgar Square. The style of the building, with its Corinthian columns and neoclassical façade, was novel for its period and had a significant influence on the subsequent development of British architecture. Today, the church is the venue for

St Martin-in-the-Fields.

St Martin-in-the-Fields, the parish church of Buckingham Palace, acts as a soup kitchen for the homeless.

Charing Cross is the official geographical centre of London. A bronze plaque marks the spot.

weekly concerts. Continuing down towards the river, enjoy a stroll along the quayside and in the beautiful gardens on **Victoria Embankment** (opened in 1870). All along the embankment, street lamps are decorated with dolphins and benches have supports in the form of camels. **Cleopatra's Needle**, an Egyptian granite obelisk, dates from 1500 BC.

Walking down towards the River Thames from Trafalgar Square, the visitor will come to Charing Cross Station, one of the largest in London. On the station forecourt stands the Eleanor Cross, a copy of one of the 12 crosses erected by Edward I to mark the funeral route of his wife, Eleanor of Castile, who died in 1290.

Throughout the year, Covent Garden is a hive of activity. Originally designed to hold a wholesale fruit and vegetable market, it is now full of small shops and craft stalls.

Street artists often perform in front of St Paul's Church in Covent Garden.

The Strand and Covent Garden

Once the centre of London's theatreland, the Strand is now more famous for being a busy thoroughfare leading to Charing Cross Station. Those who prefer shopping

In the 16th century, when it was no more than a track, members of the aristocracy built grand private houses along the Strand. In the 18th and 19th centuries, these aristocrats were replaced by bourgeois residents who built shops and theatres.

should leave the main road and head for the covered market of Covent Garden.

This pub sign shows the Duke of Wellington who is best remembered for his victory over Napoleon at the Battle of Waterloo in 1815.

An art deco building on John Adam Street.

Many of the town houses, such as the Adelphi, that were built along the Strand by the Adam brothers in the 18th century were unfortunately demolished and replaced by more modern buildings in 1938.

John and Robert Adam gave their name to a style of architecture that combines Renaissance and classical influences.

With theatres such as the Strand, the Adelphi and the Vaudeville, this area can almost compete with Shaftesbury Avenue as the capital of London's theatreland. The Savoy Hotel also has its own theatre.

Back in the 18th century, the Strand and surrounding area was a centre of entertainment, filled with theatres at which plays and musicals were performed. Today this wide thoroughfare running from Fleet Street to Charing Cross Station is lined mostly with offices and eateries and is constantly filled with taxis and people making their way to the station.

Somerset House is now home to the Courtauld Institute Galleries.

Of the large town houses owned by the aristocracy that once lined the Strand, only **Somerset House** remains. Dating from the end of the 18th century, it is the oldest surviving Georgian house in London and, since 1990, has housed the **Courtauld Institute** and its exhibitions of paintings, silverware and other works of art.

Art lovers should take time to visit the Courtauld Institute Galleries whose collection includes some famous French Impressionist paintings.

Next to the Savoy (opened in 1889), this building, an example of the inter-war style of architecture and was originally the Cecil Hotel. It is now the headquarters of Shell-Mex, the multinational oil company.

This former fruit and vegetable market is a pleasant place in which to wander.

Away from the Strand, in a maze of narrow streets, lies **Covent Garden**. This former covered market, renovated in a style that combines the old and the new, was reopened in 1980. It is now filled with antique shops, restaurants and

A relaxed friendly atmosphere perrades the cafés, restaurants and shops that fill the great hall and arcades of Covent Garden.

clothes shops around market stalls selling various arts and crafts. On the Piazza, all manner of street performers and busking musicians vie for the attention of passers-by.

The Royal Opera House is the home of the Royal Opera and the Royal Ballet. In 1892, it was the setting for the London premiere of Wagner's Ring, conducted by Gustav Mahler.

The Theatre Royal, Drury Lane

The first theatre to be built in Drury Lane was completed in 1663 and was one of only two licensed playhouses at that time in London. It was closed down in 1665 as a result of the plague that ravaged the city. During the course of its history, it has been rebuilt three times, once by the famous architect Sir Christopher Wren, and has been damaged by fire on many occasions. In the 18th century, the actor David Garrick, who took over the management of the theatre, performed in numerous productions of plays by Shakespeare, as did Edmund Kean in the 19th century. The present theatre, built by Benjamin Wyatt, was completed in 1812. A colonnade was added to the façade in 1831.

The **Royal Opera House**, near Covent Garden, represents the pinnacle of British opera. The original opera house was built in the 18th century, and was succeeded by two later buildings. The present opera house, the work of Edward Barry, was completed in 1858 and is renowned for its exceptionally good acoustics. The **Theatre Royal Drury Lane**, with its entrance in Catherine Street, is one of London's largest playhouses and supposedly one of the most haunted. At the beginning of the 19th century, it was well-known for its pantomimes but today specializes in musicals.

The Royal Courts of Justice, completed in 1882, in brick clad with Portland stone, are the country's main civil courts dealing with civil cases and appeals.

The entire history of the British legal system is concentrated in this area.

Temple

The area of London known as Temple was traditionally occupied by the journalistic and legal professions. Whilst the majority of journalists now work elsewhere, lawyers at every level of the British legal system still populate this historic area.

For over two centuries, the pubs of Fleet Street were the preserve of journalists and lawyers. Today, most newspapers have moved to more spacious locations. The Times, for example, is, like many others, now located in the Docklands.

The entrance to Middle Temple, with its ornate reliefs and statues.

Founded in the 12th century on the site of a building belonging to the Knights Templar, Temple comprises two of the four **Inns of Court** (legal institutions) of London: Middle and Inner Temple, where Mahatma Ghandi (1869–1948),

Above: A pub sign. Left: The Old Curiosity Shop is one of the oldest shops in London. It dates from the 17th century and miraculously survived the Great Fire of 1666.

once studied. This area also takes in **St Clement Danes**, the church of the Royal Air Force, and the **Royal Courts of Justice**, the country's main civil law courts.

Wigs and legal tradition

The rotunda of Temple Church has been restored on several occasions, including work to repair bomb damage suffered during World War II.

For law students, lunch hour is signalled by the sound of a horn. In the area around Temple, tradition is immutable and lawyers are still to be seen dressed in their wigs and black robes. Since they may be called to court at any time of day, many lawyers dress in black every day. **Temple Church**, the only vestige of the age of the Knights Templar, has a distinctive circular nave and combines Romanesque and Gothic elements. It has been restored on many occasions but still contains 14th-century effigies of Knights Templar. It once also served as a meeting place for barristers and their clients.

In and around Temple, magistrates and barristers can be seen in the wigs and robes that they wear during court hearings. When the courts are in session, it is sometimes possible to sit in the public gallery and follow a case being heard in the Royal Courts of Justice. Judges, dressed in red robes, direct the cases and barristers, in black robes, speak for either the defence or the prosecution. This dress code, rooted in tradition, gives hearings something of a theatrical atmosphere. Similarly, while strolling around Lincoln's Inn Fields, you are likely to spot lawyers in full regalia hurrying back to chambers, with a bundle of documents tucked under their arm.

Lincoln's Inn numbers among its former law students Cromwell, the poet John Donne and William Penn, founder of the American state of Pennsylvania.

Temple Bar, today replaced by a memorial, was a monumental gateway that marked the western limit of the City of London. Until 1772, the heads of executed criminals were displayed on this gateway.

The statue of Sir Thomas More (1478–1535) on Carey Street. The humanist and author of Utopia *was Lord Chancellor to Henry VIII until, opposed to the king's divorce, he was condemned to death and executed.*

The entrance to Lincoln's Inn.

Lincoln's Inn is the only one of the four Inns of Court that retains it original appearance, with examples of 16th, 17th and 18th century architecture which escaped the wartime bombing. On the right of Lincoln's Inn stands an early 17th-century Gothic chapel. Ben Jonson, the poet and dramatist, a contemporary of William Shakespeare, who trained as a

Stone Buildings, on the north side of New Square, date from 1774 to 1780.

bricklayer, was involved in its construction. Past the chapel lies **Lincoln's Inn Fields**, the largest square in London where public executions once took place. Nearby is the attractive **Sir John Soane Museum.** Further to the north are the gardens of **Gray's Inn**, the only gardens of the four Inns of Court that are open to the public.

The Royal Courts of Justice were originally at Westminster. They were transferred to their present location in the 19th century so as to be nearer the Inns of Court.

Lincoln's Inn Fields is lined with a number of attractive brick buildings. Among them is Great Hall (pictured above) which now has additional stucco decoration on its façade.

Street artists installed at the entrances to Leicester Square offer portraits or caricatures drawn from life.

T he heart of the capital is full of contrasts, from peaceful squares and museums to crowded shops, theatres, bars and restaurants.

A half-timbered mock-Tudor façade.

The Heart of London

Highly fashionable in the 19th century, Russell Square became a sought-after address for wealthy businessmen and lawyers in the early 20th century.

The British Museum and University of London lend a studious air to the area.

Bloomsbury

The discreet elegant streets of Bloomsbury, with their beautiful Georgian architecture, bask in an atmosphere of literature and art. Its main landmarks, the imposing British Museum and the University of London, are steeped in intellectual tradition.

The long garden in Tavistock Square is surrounded by elegant houses dating from 1806–1826, the work of Thomas Cubitt (1788-1855). This English builder was also responsible for the east façade of Buckingham Palace.

Russell Square, laid out in 1800, was once home to wealthy businessmen.

No. 48 Doughty Street, in the very heart of Bloomsbury, is the house where Charles Dickens lived during the most productive years of his life. Within those walls, between 1837 and 1839, he penned *Oliver Twist*, *Nicholas Nickleby* and *The Adventures of Mr Pickwick*. A plaque in Bloomsbury Square, one of the oldest squares in London, honours the area's most illustrious inhabitants. Bloomsbury was the

The University of London grew out of University College, which was founded in 1826 in Gower Street. Since then, the university has expanded into large areas of Bloomsbury.

Charles Dickens' House

Charles Dickens (1812–70) is one of the most popular English novelists in the world. Although he came from a humble background, he was famous by the age of 25 through his book *The Adventures of Mr Pickwick* (1837). He owned several houses in London, but the one in Doughty Street is the only one still standing today. It was purchased by the Friends of Charles Dickens in 1923 and turned into a museum. Inside, it is as if time has stood still; the house is arranged as it would have been in Dickens' day, with manuscripts, letters, portraits, and furniture brought from his other London houses. The museum also holds a number of first editions of his works.

The Russell Hotel, overlooking Russell Square, was built in 1900, in late-Victorian style. Its façade is clad with ceramic tiles.

area inhabited and frequented by the British intelligentsia of the late 19th and early 20th centuries. The Bloomsbury Group, centred around the novelist Virginia Woolf, included such eminent figures as the poet T.S. Eliot and Sigmund Freud, the founder of psychoanalysis. Meanwhile, near Fitzroy Square, the writer Aldous Huxley, the philosopher Bertrand Russell and the dancer Vaslav Nijinski would meet at Lady Ottoline Morrell's. The green expanse of **Russell Square** is overlooked by the University of London, founded in 1836 by royal charter.

Beneath the great dome of the British Library's Reading Room, Karl Marx, Lenin and Kipling put the finishing touches to their writings.

The Mexican Room at the British Museum.

The Rosetta Stone, discovered in the Nile Delta in 1799, is on permanent display at the British Museum. It helped the French Egyptologist Jean-François Champollion to decipher Egyptian hieroglyphic script, which he succeeded in doing in 1822.

Ranging from prehistoric Europe to the Middle Ages, and from ancient Egypt to Oriental antiquities and the art of ancient Mexico, the British Museum's archaeological collections are stunningly diverse.

The **British Museum**, founded in 1753, seems rather daunting at first glance. It would probably take a week to discover all the riches that are displayed in the rooms of this vast museum. Its collection of Egyptian and Greek antiquities is without doubt among the largest and best known in the world. Part of that collection consists of the Elgin Marbles from

The imposing façade of the British Museum.

the Parthenon, brought back from Athens by Lord Elgin at the beginning of the 19th century and bought for the museum by the government. The **British Library** contains some 18 million volumes and was once adjacent to the British Museum; it is now housed in a modern building on St Pancras, to the north of the museum.

Among the 7 million objects brought back by explorers between the 17th and the 19th centuries are many of those making up the impressive collection of Egyptian antiquities. The displays include many pieces discovered during Napoleon's Egyptian Expedition of 1799 and handed over to Britain after the Treaty of Alexandria of 1801.

The façade of Selfridges, built at the beginning of the 20th century. Along with Harrod's, it is one of the smartest department stores in London.

Roads leading on to Oxford Street are often congested.

Oxford Street, Soho and Piccadilly

Oxford Street, the longest shopping street in London, is flanked to the south by the area of Soho, which retains something of its notoriety as a red-light district.

The Metropolitan Police, distinguishable by their helmets marked with the royal crown, have their headquarters at Scotland Yard. Their nickname 'Bobbies', is derived from Sir Robert (Bobby) Peel, who established the force in 1829.

Nearby, the kaleidoscopic neon signs of Piccadilly light up the night sky.

Oxford Street is not a place for those who don't like crowds!

Oxford Street, 1 mile (2.5 kilometres) long, follows an ancient Roman road. In times gone by, it was the route taken by condemned criminals on their way from the Tower of London to the gallows at Tyburn (now Marble Arch). Today the street is a shopper's paradise where you will find the likes of Marks & Spencer, the Body Shop, John Lewis

Britain is above all else famous for its pubs and beer. Traditional English beer is known as 'ale'. 'Bitter' is an ale with a sharper flavour, whilst 'pale ale' has a more subtle taste. Dark ales include 'stout' and 'mild', which is paler

than the former. Draught beer is normally served by the pint (0.56 litres) but can also be ordered in half-pint measures.

The façade of Liberty's.

The traditional red phone boxes owned by British Telecom (BT) are now joined by more modern orange models owned by New World.

and Selfridge's. Just below Oxford Street, on the corner of Regent Street and Great Marlborough Street, stands Liberty's. Founded in 1875, this store still sells the fabrics and Oriental silks that made it famous. The present mock-Tudor building dates from 1925. Smaller specialized shops can be found on nearby Regent Street and Bond Street.

Selfridges was the first department store to open in London. It was also the first to be built with a visible steel skeleton.

The shop signs of Virgin Megastore and HMV Records remind visitors that London is the capital of rock. A victim of its own success, shopping in Oxford Street is not the most pleasant of experiences in the period leading up to Christmas!

Carnaby Street, once the home of 1960's fashion, is now largely given over to the tourist market.

Pubs bedecked with flowers and greenery bring a rural air to the centre of the city.

Soho, not far from these smart shops, upholds its reputation as the red-light district of London. Bordered by Carnaby Street, Charing Cross Road and Chinatown, it was once a hotbed of prostitution but, after World War II, residents joined forces to have most of the sex shops closed down. Since then, Soho has been a popular

Soho Square is at the very heart of London's music, film and television industries, which have taken over a large area of Soho. The square (dating from 1681) is laid out with lawns and contains a guardian's lodge that was added in Victorian times.

meeting place for 'swingers' during the 60s, punks during the 70s and now the gay community.

A colourful display of fruit and vegetables at Berwick Street Market.

The foreign artists and intellectuals who chose to live in Soho, alongside communities of Greek, Italian and French immigrants, included the young Mozart, the painter Canaletto and Karl Marx and his family. Today, the streets of Soho are frequented by the young and fashionable, who come to be seen in its many cafés and restaurants. The latter stock up on their supplies in **Berwick Street Market**.

Soho has always been the most cosmopolitan area of the capital, attracting immigrants due to its cheap rents.

*Having origi-
nally settled
near the docks of
the East End, the
Chinese commu-
nity moved to
Soho in the
1950s.*

The multitude of French, Italian, Greek and Chinese restaurants off Soho Square offers visitors a truly cosmopolitan choice of menu. **Chinatown**, which covers the southern part of Soho around Gerrard Street, is a microcosm of exoticism. Entering this district, the visitor passes through a pair of Chinese gates and steps into a world where rows of roast ducks are displayed in shop windows and where medicinal herbs are bought and sold. The opium dens have long since gone to be replaced with the aroma of spices which evoke the atmosphere of an Oriental sea port.

From punk rock to haute couture

Before she became the high priestess of British haute couture and opened shops in exclusive Mayfair, Vivienne Westwood was one of the original punks. In partnership with the producer Malcolm MacLaren in the 1970s, she helped launch the subversive Sex Pistols, a band who were to inspire a social, cultural and musical revolution among a disaffected generation of young people. Having made the safety pin and the nose ring a fashion statement, she has remained prominent in the public eye with her creative originality, which has since found a ready market abroad.

From the vantage point of his column, Eros has seen many changes to Piccadilly Circus over the years.

The fountain in Piccadilly Circus.

Even late at night, there is an endless flow of people wandering through the shopping arcades or making their way to theatres and restaurants.

Leicester Square can be reached by cutting through Coventry Street. At the heart of London's theatreland, the square attracts large numbers of tourists with its many souvenir shops, discotheques and wide-screen cinemas where film premieres are often held.

Erected in 1893 in the middle of **Piccadilly Circus**, the bronze statue of the angel of charity (now known as Eros) commemorates the good work done by the minister and philanthropist Lord Shaftesbury. The amount of traffic that builds up around this square, lit night and day by flashing neon signs, means that the wise would do well to leave their cars at home!

The Piccadilly Theatre is just one of the many theatres on Shaftesbury Avenue.

In 1981, as befits an area dedicated to film and theatre, a statue of Charlie Chaplin by John Doubleday was erected in the little garden at the centre of **Leicester Square**. Having said hello to Charlie, visitors can then go on to pay their respects to Shakespeare, whose statue, a few steps away, is a replica of the one that stands in Westminster Abbey.

In Piccadilly Circus, be sure to visit the latest attraction, the Rock Circus in what was once the London Pavilion. It is a branch of Mme Tussaud's and covers more than 40 years of rock and pop, from Elvis Presley to Michael Jackson and James Brown. See the legendary figures of rock whilst listening to their songs through a stereo headset.

Grand terraces of Victorian houses, with imposing doorways, are to be seen in Belgravia. This exclusive residential area is the preserve of the very rich.

A number of rich fashionable districts, like small villages, cover a large area of London between Hyde Park and the Thames.

The rules of Chester Square Gardens.

London's Villages

A surprising facet of London is the contrast between city life and the almost village-like atmosphere of certain other areas. As London developed during the 19th century, it engulfed outlying villages, many of which were in the middle of the countryside. Some of these villages have retained their identity. Visitors can buy home-made jam, walk along towpaths or enjoy a drink in a pub on the riverbank. At the opposite end of the scale, some of London's villages are highly exclusive enclaves, inhabited only by the very rich.

The shops in the Burlington Arcade offer a wealth of beautiful clothes, shoes, jewellery and other exquisite objects. The arcade itself is patrolled by uniformed beadles.

Mayfair and St James's

Located between Piccadilly and Park Lane, the small residential district of Mayfair is one of the most aristocratic areas of London. High society is also to be found in St James's, which basks in the glory of its royal associations.

London's most prestigious clothes shops are concentrated around Mayfair. Only the lucky few, however, can afford the expensive cashmeres on offer, or the clothes carrying the labels of top international designers.

The Burlington Arcade is lined with small shops specializing in luxury goods.

Mayfair takes its name from the May Fair that began there in 1668, a fair at which animals and cereals were bought and sold. The area attracted the attention of the Dukes of Westminster who trans-formed it, building grand town houses and squares.

Those hoping to enjoy afternoon tea in the luxurious setting of the Palm Court of the Ritz will need to book a few weeks in advance and follow the strict dress code.

Even though little remains of these 17th and 18th-century houses (with the exception of **Crew House**, in Curzon Street), the area retains its aristocratic atmosphere.

Crew House, a town house in Curzon Street, is just one of the beautiful buildings that lend Mayfair its air of luxury and elegance.

Shepherd Market, densely packed with an interesting variety of restaurants, antique shops and delicatessens, is named after Edward Shepherd who built it in the mid-18th century on the site of the former May Fair. The district was once home to such illustrious figures as the poet Lord Byron, and the prime minister Gladstone. Along Davies Street lies **Grosvenor Square** with its garden, laid out by Edward Shepherd in 1725. Of the original buldings, only two remain, one of which was used by John Adams during his time as minister to England (1785-1788) before he became president.

Queen Elizabeth II

Mayfair, which boasts many impressive town houses and illustrious residents, was also the birthplace of Queen Elizabeth II. The future queen was born in 1926 at 17 Burton Street, east of Berkeley Square, near the delightful gardens where nightingales once sang.

The daughter of George VI, she married Prince Philip of Greece, later Duke of Edinburgh, in 1947. On the death of her father in February 1952, she acceded to the throne and at her coronation in Westminster Abbey in 1953, she was formally proclaimed Queen of the United Kingdom of Great Britain and Northern Ireland. She is also the head of the Commonwealth and of the Church of England.

At Fortnum and Mason's, the society grocers, the clock on the façade has models that perform the Changing of the Guard every hour.

The Café Royal, (1865), was regularly frequented by the painters Whistler, the illustrator Aubrey Beardsley and the writer Oscar Wilde.

A quiet street in the heart of Mayfair.

The **Museum of Mankind** at 6 Burlington Gardens is well worth a visit. It has exceptionally rich and varied ethnographic collections, largely due to the fact that London was once the capital of a great seafaring nation. The museum was built in 1866–1867 and in its galleries are displayed tribal art from Africa, the Pacific and the Americas.

The permanent collection on display at the Royal Academy of Arts includes works by Michelangelo, Constable and Turner. At its Summer Exhibition, paintings, drawings and sculptures are displayed by established names as well as up-and-coming artists.

St James's Street is lined with shops displaying cashmere clothes, silverware and jewellery. The window display of Hugh Johnson's is shown here.

Tea time is a British institution that can still be enjoyed in many of the capital's cafés and hotels.

By royal appointment: The royal warrant is awarded to official suppliers to the Crown. The royal coat of arms is a guarantee of quality and craftsmanship.

Lobb's, shoemakers to the Queen.

Floris, purveyors of perfumes and toiletries, was founded in 1730. The shop is now located in Jermyn Street, a narrow street near St James's Street. In the past, it has supplied famous customers such as Queen Victoria and the writer Oscar Wilde.

As well as its annual Summer Exhibition, the **Royal Academy of Arts,** opposite the Ritz Hotel, mounts many major temporary exhibitions and is also an important art school. On the opposite side of Piccadilly, Fortnum and Mason's, founded in 1707, displays the royal coat of arms, indicating that it as an official supplier to Her Majesty the Queen.

Lock & Co, a milliner's since 1759, has premises at No. 6 St James's Street.

The majestic **Café Royal** fits in perfectly with the many luxurious shopping arcades of Piccadilly. Lobb's Bespoke Bootmakers supply the Queen and number among their former customers Sir Winston Churchill and Frank Sinatra. Lovers of fine cheeses and Scottish delicacies should visit Paxton & Whitfield, in nearby Jermyn Street.

Ever since King Charles II made St James's Palace his home in the 17th century, this area of London has basked in the reflected glory of royalty. It was here, during that period, that gentlemen's clubs were established. These typically British institutions have their own strict set of rules and allow only a small, very select number of members...all men, of course.

Belgrave Square epitomizes the rather formal character of Belgravia, to the south of Hyde Park. This is in complete contrast to the more relaxed feel of Chelsea.

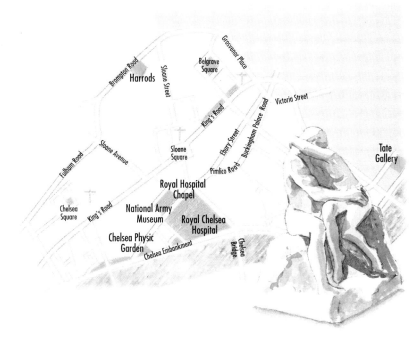

Belgravia and Chelsea

Belgravia has shared the wealth and upper-class atmosphere of Mayfair since the early 19th century, whilst Chelsea, the traditional haunt of artists, is rather more relaxed and friendly, with an almost

The development of Belgravia began in the 1820s, when Lord Grosvenor, a wealthy landowner, decided to build on his land. This he did in partnership with the Master of Public Works, Thomas Cubitt.

village-like atmosphere.

Harrod's once boasted that it could supply anything, even an elephant! Even though that is no longer true, the store still offers a very impressive range.

At night, 11,500 bulbs light up the shop front of Harrod's, the world-famous department store.

Harrod's, located in Knightsbridge, is worth a visit as much for the splendour of its decoration and displays as for the quality and the variety of the goods on offer. It is hard to believe that the store began as a humble grocer's, opened by Henry Charles Harrod in 1849.

Harrod's on Brompton Road.

Belgravia is an area of large town houses and wide avenues. The houses around Belgrave Square, with their entrances framed by neoclassical columns, are owned by the rich and famous. Towards Knightsbridge and South Kensington, property prices are so high that the area is largely taken up by public buildings and the offices of multinational companies.

The Tate Gallery is named after Sir Henry Tate, a philanthropic patron of the arts.

The **Tate Gallery**, which overlooks the Thames on Millbank, was opened in 1897 and contains a rich collection of British painting from the 16th century to the present day, including works by painters such as Hogarth, Gainsborough, Constable, Blake and Turner. It also has a large collection of modern art and sculptures.

With works by artists such as Matisse, Picasso, Dali, Lucian Freud and Francis Bacon, the Tate Gallery is the largest museum of modern art in London. Only a small part (just one sixth) of its collection is on public display at any one time. The Clore Gallery, a modern wing of the Tate Gallery devoted entirely to Turner, is of international renown.

Pubs are open from 11 am to 11 pm Monday to Saturday, and 12 noon to 10.30 pm on Sundays. When the barman calls time, drinkers have ten minutes to finish their drinks.

Chelsea Flower Show, which takes place in May in the gardens of the Royal Hospital, is attended by the Queen.

At 81 Fulham Road, Michelin House still has its original mosaics. The upper floor is now the Bibendum restaurant where stained-glass windows still depict the rotund

A terrace of Victorian houses.

Away from the main thoroughfares, the side streets of Chelsea, on the banks of the Thames, enjoy an almost village-like atmosphere. Wander through this charming district and imagine the lives of the many writers and artists who made the area their home, including Turner, George Eliot, T S Eliot and Ian Fleming.

Michelin man. Working out at around £50 per person, diners on a tight budget may want to find somewhere slightly cheaper!

The writer George Eliot, whose real name was Mary Ann Evans (1819–1880), lived at 4 Cheyne Walk, one of the most attractive streets in London.

The Royal Hospital, built in red brick and white Portland stone.

The famous Royal Hospital is home to some 400 retired soldiers, known as Chelsea Pensioners. They wear a distinctive uniform: dark trousers, with a scarlet tunic in summer and a dark blue tunic in winter.

A fine example of Georgian architecture is to be seen in the houses lining **Cheyne Walk**, where the painter Dante Gabriel Rossetti and the American novelist Henry James once lived. From the **Chelsea Physic Garden**, a 17th-century walled garden renowned for its medicinal plants, to the **Royal Hospital**, built by Christopher Wren during the reign of Charles II, the Thames embankment is a pleasant place for a stroll.

The King's Road is a shopping street popular with the fashionable and wealthy set.

Turning back towards Sloane Square, the visitor will come to the **Royal Court Theatre**, which specializes in avant-garde productions. The **King's Road**, leading off the western side of the square, was the birthplace of swing and hippie culture in the 1960s and of the punk movement of the 1970s; it is now filled with fashionable clothes outlets, cafés and antique shops.

Beyond the King's Road, blue ceramic plaques on houses that line the web of narrow streets mark the residences of the many artists, writers and other famous people who once lived in Chelsea. Those with a love of antiques can wander through the King's Road's three antiques markets: Antiquarius, the Chenil Galleries and the Chelsea Antiques Market.

The imposing façade of the Natural History Museum, with its monumental entrance, is an institution dedicated to scientific knowledge.

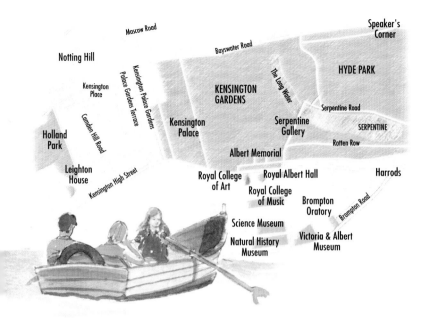

Kensington

Kensington is the Mecca of culture with one of the highest concentrations of museums in the world. It is the result of Prince Albert's desire to create a

Before the 17th century, Kensington was little more than a village on the outskirts of London. The western part of this district, which is almost entirely residential, consists of Victorian houses and green open spaces that give it an almost rural atmosphere.

centre of scientific and artistic knowledge in the heart of the capital.

This dinosaur skeleton stands in the entrance hall of the Natural History Museum.

Ever since it was opened in 1881, the buildings and collections of the **Natural History Museum** have been the object of general admiration. It is both a museum and a research centre and has an exceptionally good library. Its rich collections cover

The western side of Kensington, towards Holland Park, is largely residential, consisting of many large elegant town houses.

several disciplines (palaeontology, zoology, entomology, botany and mineralogy) and its modern interactive displays are sure to fascinate visitors of any age.

The façade of the Victoria & Albert Museum is built in a mock 16th-century Franco-Flemish style. The museum possesses the world's largest collection of Indian artefacts outside Asia.

Natural history and science

Using traditional displays and the latest technology, the Natural History Museum introduces the visitor to such diverse subjects as zoology (with the whale gallery), palaeontology (with the dinosaurs gallery) and the history of the Earth. With 67 million objects and over one million books and manuscripts, this is the largest natural history collection in the world, employing more than 300 scientists and archivists to work behind the scenes. The Science Museum, round the corner in Exhibition Road, exhibits great inventions and technological feats, from steam engines to spacecraft. The Imperial College of Science and Technology, meanwhile, is noted for producing engineers of renown.

The **Victoria & Albert Museum,** popularly known as the V & A, also stands on Cromwell Road. It was founded by Prince Albert after the Great Exhibition of 1851 but was not completed until 1909. As the national museum of both fine and applied arts, it contains objects from all over the world, including large collections of furniture, paintings, costumes, ceramics and silverware, dating from the Renaissance to the 20th century. This extraordinary museum is also unique in the fact that it exhibits five centuries of British art in one building.

The Royal Albert Hall is decorated with a terracotta frieze.

Right: The Albert
Memorial, erected
near the spot
where the Great
Exhibition of
1851 took place,
honours the
memory of Queen
Victoria's consort,
Prince Albert of
Saxe-Coburg-
Gotha (1819–
1861). The Albert
Hall, an elliptical
amphitheatre in
the Italian Renaissance style, is 180 feet (55
metres) high and a tribute to the prince's love
of art, culture and science.

The **Royal Albert Hall**, in
the heart of Kensington, was
completed in 1871. Its façade
of red brick is decorated
with a terracotta frieze sym-
bolizing the triumph of arts
and science. This spacious
amphitheatre is not only used
for classical concerts, but also
conferences and boxing
matches. Further along,
Leighton House, home of

Imperial College of Science & Technology.

The Royal College of Music, opposite the Royal Albert Hall, is open to the public on Wednesdays. Exhibits include Handel's spinet and a clavichord owned by Haydn.

the Pre-Raphaelite painter Lord Leighton, is remarkable for its Victorian decor. The Arab-Hall was added in 1879 for its owner's collection of Islamic tiles. The paintings on display in the reception rooms include a number by Leighton himself. **Holland Park,** nearby, is leafier than neighbouring areas and has several small public gardens and squares.

The Japanese garden in Holland Park was laid out in 1991 as part of the London Festival of Japan.

Holland House has been altered several times since it was built in 1670. It was badly damaged during the war so that little of the original building has survived. In contrast, many of the Victorian houses on the edges of Holland Park are original and stand as prime examples of the architecture of that period.

Many traditional British telephone boxes like these have now been replaced by newer models which take coins or phonecards.

For a welcome break from the bustle of city life, explore London's villages and canals between the slopes of Notting Hill and Camden Market.

The logo of London Underground.

Away from the Centre

Away from the city's monuments and classic landmarks, another face of London awaits to be discovered. Little Venice, Regent's Park, London Zoo, the Wallace Collection, the Docklands, the open-air markets at Portobello and Camden Lock are all equally well worth a visit. In Camden Market, traders set up their makeshift stalls in front of colourful shop façades. They may be there one day and gone the next, depending on the number of police sweeps of the area.

The Notting Hill Carnival, established by the West Indian community in 1966, is spread over three days. On the third day, the festivities reach a peak, with the arrival of the Rastafarians. Traditional British reserve is swept aside as steel bands play and Jamaican rum flows. Some 40,000 people dance to a reggae or jungle beat that booms out from powerful sound systems. Lest things get out of hand, the carnival takes place under the watchful eye of 'bobbies'.

One of the many art galleries.

Notting Hill, in west London, became fashionable in the 1980s, and the avant-garde art galleries and antique shops that were opened there are now well established. The mix of Victorian terraces, grand 18th-century mansions and more modest though colourful housing is quite in keeping with the diversity of this district. For those

Once a year, the lively, cosmopolitan streets of Notting Hill are taken over by the West Indian carnival. This event, the largest open-air festival in Europe, takes place over three days. The floats are the first on the scene. Then a multitude of dancers, performing to live music, fill the streets with sound and colour.

The colourful stalls of Portobello Market present a mesmerizing display.

interested in antiques and jewellery, the well-attended market on **Portobello Road**, established in 1837, is an essential port of call. Packed with bargain-hunters, this is not for the faint-hearted, but is an unusually friendly place and is worth a visit to experience all that this unique flea market has to offer.

The stallholders in Portobello Market, whether selling jewellery, antique silverware or clothes, have a reputation for sticking to their asking prices, so haggling may get you nowhere. Continuing north-ward, you will come to the plaque (left) that marks the boundary with the borough of Paddington, a district that has other surprises in store...

Little Venice takes its name from the network of canals that wind through the area.

Further north, in the borough of **Paddington**, where the **Grand Union Canal** widens into a large basin, nestles London's watery jewel: **Little Venice**, the name given by Lord Byron to this network of canals. It is a favourite area with Londoners and, wandering along the towpaths that border the canals, it is easy to see why. Many canal boats, painted in bright colours, often serve as second homes

Well-kept and brightly-painted canal boats are often comfortably fitted out and attractively decorated. Lace curtains can even be seen hanging at the brass portholes.

Madame Tussaud's and the London Planetarium

Although the railways brought about the end of canal transport, canals have now been given a new lease of life. Tourists can take a trip in mini-barges or enjoy a walk along the old towpaths.

Madame Tussaud was a prominent figure at the court of Louis XVI who began modelling in wax when she was imprisoned during the French Revolution. To avoid being executed, she made models of the heads of prominent victims of the guillotine. Having arrived in London in 1802, carrying 35 wax masks, she founded Madame Tussaud's Exhibition at the age of 74. To this day, the wax models of people from the worlds of music, show business, politics and sport are made following traditional methods. With a collection of several hundred wax models and a Chamber of Horrors, Madame Tussaud's is one of London's most popular attractions. The London Planetarium and its celestial vault is next door.

or, for some lucky owners, as permanent floating residences. Some of these 'home sweet homes' are rented out and command amazingly high prices. The former working canal has today been transformed into a leisure amenity and mini-barges can be hired for trips between Little Venice and **Camden Lock**. As the journey progresses, 19th-century houses to the left and right of the canals give way to the green landscape of Regent's Park, home to London Zoo. Opened in 1828, the zoo can be reached via the canal, using the loading stage situated next to it.

Every school of European painting is represented at the Wallace Collection.

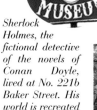

Sherlock Holmes, the fictional detective of the novels of Conan Doyle, lived at No. 221b Baker Street. His world is recreated in the Sherlock Holmes Museum, between Nos. 237 and 239 Baker Street.

Portman Square was laid out by Robert Adam in the second half of the 18th century.

The **Wallace Collection**, one of the finest private art collections in the world, was formed by the 4th Earl of Hertford and his heir, Sir Richard Wallace who bequeathed it to the nation in 1897. The collection in Hertford House, their private residence, includes many 17th and 18th-century paintings by such artists as Rembrandt, Velasquez, Rubens, Boucher and Fragonard, as well as porcelain and other works of art.

In The Laughing Cavalier *(1624), the Dutch painter Frans Hals captures the ironic expression of his 26-year-old model.*

Queen Mary's Gardens are a riot of colour.

In summer, plays by Shakespeare are performed in the Inner Circle and rose gardens of Queen Mary's Gardens, in the middle of Regent's Park.

London's huge mosque, conspicuous by its brass dome and minaret, stands to the west of Regent's Park.

Primrose Hill, which rises to an altitude of 200 feet (62 metres), dominates Regent's Park, commanding views over London. An orientation table on the top of the hill enables the city's major landmarks to be identified. In winter, tobogganers can be seen speeding down the hill's snow-covered slopes, while in summer this grassy vantage point is the ideal spot for family picnics. Turning back northward along Baker Street, take time to

The eight surviving Nash terraces have been converted into luxury flats.

visit **Regent's Park**, an area of greenery that is much less formally laid out than Hyde Park. In 1811, the future King Geroge IV commissioned his favourite architect, John Nash, to build private houses and a summer palace on ancient hunting grounds used by Henry VIII. Due to lack of funds, however, this ambitious project was never completed and the country's first ever 'garden city' was then transformed into a public park. Today, to the east and west of the park, a number of of Regency-style buildings, known as the Nash terraces, are all that remain.

London Zoo, one of the oldest institutions in the city, is currently suffering from low attendance. It houses 1162 species of animals and, to counter the negative image of zoos, now stresses the part that it plays in the protection of endangered species.

In Camden Market, street vendors selling hand-crafted jewellery and second-hand furniture display their wares in front of colourfully painted stores.

On Camden Market's official stalls, nearly-new and second-hand clothes can be found along with old records and natural remedies.

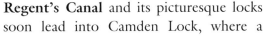

The crowds of Camden Market.

Some forms of headgear are as striking as any worn by Her Majesty the Queen.

Regent's Canal and its picturesque locks soon lead into Camden Lock, where a lively flea market is held. **Camden Market** has grown considerably since it was established and now rivals Portobello Market in size. It became very fashionable in the early 1980s and still draws a motley crowd of bargain-hunters, particularly at the weekend.

In this area of London, no one bats an eyelid at unconventional lifestyles and unusual fashions. These tartans suits, for example, may not be to everyone's taste, but Camden is a place where anything goes!

Lambeth Palace, on the south bank of the Thames, was built between 1207 and 1229. For seven and half centuries it has been the residence of the Archbishops of Canterbury.

London has been flooded several times in the course of its history; the worst being in 1883 and 1937.

Goods imported from every corner of the British Empire were first stored in the tall warehouses of the Docklands, well out of sight of prying eyes. Many of these warehouses have now been converted into luxury apartments.

The Isle of Dogs and Canary Wharf.

When London was still a major port, the Thames was the scene of constant activity and enormous **docks** were built to accommodate the increasing volume of traffic on the river. At the beginning of the 20th century, almost 21,000 people were employed in the ship-building industry. Later, however, shipping firms deserted **Greenwich**, which

A view of London's docks where new developments are taking shape.

was badly bombed during World War II. Then in the early 1980s, an ambitious programme of redevelopment began. The ultra-modern skyscrapers of the financial and media worlds that tower over the old warehouses on the **Isle of Dogs** (reputedly once the training ground of royal hounds) is just one aspect of this regeneration.

The meridian passes through the Greenwich Observatory, founded by King Charles II in 1675.

The Docklands area of London, largely destroyed and deserted during World War II, has recently undergone major redevelopment. Modern steel and glass buildings now stand next to converted warehouses.

Greenwich has for centuries been at the heart of Britain's maritime power.

Right: Elegant tall ships, such as the Cutty Sark, are moored in Tobacco Dock where they are open to the public. The Cutty Sark was originally used in the 19th century to bring cargoes of tea from the Orient.

The pace of redevelopment was, however, severely curtailed by the economic crisis of the late 1980s. Nevertheless, the Docklands is now graced by prestigious modern apartments and luxury yachts. On the south side of the river stands the **National Maritime Museum** and the **Queen's House**, the summer residence of Queen Henrietta Maria designed by Inigo Jones. As the 21st century dawns, the Docklands promise to

The Thames Barrier was built to prevent future floods.

gleam with new apartment blocks, restaurants and cafés interspersed with parks overlooking the river. The greatest project will be the **New Millennium Experience**. This will take the form of a huge concrete dome, designed by Sir Richard Rogers, covering a spacious arena capable of accommodating 10,000 people where major displays and interactive exhibitions will take place. On the river east of Greenwich lies the **Thames Barrier**. This great feat of engineering, begun in 1972 and completed in 1982, protects London from the eventuality of flooding by the Thames.

The cost of the millennium celebrations in the year 2000 has been estimated at £5.6 million, almost half of which will come from the National Lottery. Other major projects are to include improvements to the British Museum, the Tate Gallery and the South Bank Centre and a building to house the National Film Institute in the heart of the Docklands.

Creative Workshop

*Having discovered the wonders of London,
it's now time to get creative.*

*All you need are a few odds and ends and a little
ingenuity to keep the spirit of your adventure alive by
creating your own beautiful craft objects.*

*These simple yet ingenious ideas capture the special
flavour of London and leave you with
a permanent reminder of your visit.*

*An original, simple and fun way to preserve
your holiday memories.*

A Mosaic Teapot

*W*hat *could be more British than a nice cup of tea!
Brighten up an old teapot with this jazzy mosaic
design – then invite your friends round for a cuppa!*

• If possible, choose tiles of the same thickness.
• Lay out the tiles on the plank of wood and
break them into pieces with the hammer.
• Then, using the mosaic cutter, trim them
into small triangles, squares or other shapes.
Separate them into different colours.
• With the knife or spatula, spread tile cement
over one side of a teapot; make sure that the
cement forms an even layer and is not too
thick.

• Press the mosaic pieces
into the cement, starting
at the top and working
down.
• Repeat this process for
the other side and lid.
Leave the teapot to dry for
one day.
• Mix some tile grout into
a thick paste.
• With the sponge or
spatula, spread it all over
the teapot to fill all the
gaps between the mosaic
pieces.
• Now take a damp cloth
and gently wipe away the

surplus tile grout.

• With, a dry cloth, rub the teapot hard to remove any residue.

• If you have used glass mosaic, it will be more difficult to clean since this material is quite porous. The best way of getting rid of these last traces of cement is with a very dilute solution of hydrochloric acid.

• After cleaning, make sure that you rinse the teapot thoroughly under running water.

• Finally, buff the teapot with a cloth dipped in a little linseed oil.

Materials

• china teapot • a few ceramic tiles, glazed or unglazed, or some glass mosaic • mosaic cutters
• plank of wood and hammer • small amount of tile cement; this can be white, grey or coloured
• tile grout • knife or small spatula
• cloths • sponge • linseed oil

Place Markers

The designs and colours of these place markers are inspired by the famous pottery first produced by Josiah Wedgwood in the late 18th century.

- Choose your motif and trace the outline with the felt-tip pen onto a piece of Bristol board.

- Carefully cut out the motif with a Stanley knife.

- Place it on a sheet of stiff white paper, fixing it in place with sticky tape.

- Turn the paper over.

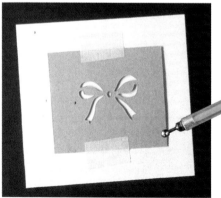

- Place it on a smooth surface and rub it with the embossing pen or knitting needle so as to make a raised imprint of the stencil. This is delicate work. Using small circular movements, press hard enough to produce a raised design on the white paper but not so hard that you risk tearing the paper.

• Gently remove the stencil and with the Stanley knife carefully cut round the raised motif, less than 0.04" (1 mm) from the embossed edge. The edges should be smooth.

• Take a sheet of card, and cut out a square measuring 4" (10 cm).

• Fold it in half. To finish your place marker, glue the embossed design near the fold in the left-hand corner of the card.

Materials

- fine felt-tip pen
- sheet of Bristol board
- sheet of stiff white paper • sheet of pale blue or green card • sticky tape
- embossing pen or blunt knitting needle
- Stanley knife
- scissors

A Plantpot Holder

The fresh colours and simple patterns of this plantpot holder will bring a breath of fresh air to your home. If you intend to use it outside, you may want to choose colours that blend in with your garden.

Two shades of green

• Wash the plantpot holder, wipe it and leave it to dry thoroughly before you begin to paint.

• Paint the inside and the outside of the pot, including the bottom, in a single colour, using the thick brush and applying the paint as evenly as possible.

• Leave it to dry.

• Then, using a darker green and the thick brush, dab paint all over the inside of the pot. Allow it to dry and repeat so as to produce a natural mottled effect.

The daisies

• Practice painting daisies on a separate sheet of paper until you can paint individual petals with a single brush stroke.

• Now start painting the pot. Use very diluted paint and apply a second coat to each petal if necessary.

• Use a strong yellow for the centre of each daisy, adding a light brushstroke in a paler colour so as to create a 3D effect.

• Leave the pot to dry before continuing.

The blue trim

• Finish off by painting the frieze. Several coats may be needed to obtain the desired shade.

• When it is dry, carefully add a white border and the green dots.

Materials

• iron plantpot holder • metal paint in several bright colours
• thick, round-ended paintbrush
• medium-fine paintbrush

A Cross-stitch Bookmark

*T*he Beefeaters guard the Crown Jewels at the Tower of London, resplendent in their distinctive uniform.

• Fold the canvas in two along its length so as to find the centre and mark this with two cross stitches.

• Starting from the centre of the canvas and the centre of the Beefeater motif, work in cross stitch, following the pattern. Always use a double thickness of thread.

• Each square in the pattern corresponds to a cross stitch. For the face, use a double strand of black thread and make the eyes by rolling the thread round the needle

twice then pushing the needle through the canvas (see diagram above).

• Use the same method for the detail on the uniform, but use a single strand of thread.

• When you have finished the Beefeater, embroider two rows of cross stitch in double thread at the top and bottom of the canvas.

• To finish the book mark, make the fringe: do this by teasing out the horizontal strands of canvas for eight rows at the top and bottom.

• Finally, press the back of the book mark with a warm iron.

Materials

• strip of white tapestry canvas 8" (20 cm) long and 2" (5 cm) wide
• embroidery silks in white, black, red, yellow ochre, pink, brown and blue
• embroidery needle

A Beef
in Beer Pie

*T*his traditional beef in beer pie
can be found on the menu at
pubs and restaurants throughout
Britain. A simple tasty dish for
a cold winter's night.

The meat and vegetables

- Cut the beef into 1 " (2 cm) cubes.
- Season the flour with salt and pepper.
- Coat the beef in the flour and place it in an oven-proof dish.
- Peel the carrot and the onion, slice them and add them to the beef.
- Mix together the beer, vinegar, sugar and stock and pour onto the beef and vegetables.

The pastry

- Thoroughly mix together all the ingredients for the pastry, adding enough water to make a dough.
- Roll out the pastry on a floured board. Cover the oven-proof dish with the pastry.
- Cover the pie with baking foil. Place the dish in the oven, preheated to 170°C (350°F, gas mark 4) and leave to bake for two and a quarter hours.
- Remove the baking foil for about 10 minutes before the end of cooking so that the pastry browns.
- Serve with vegetables.

Ingredients

To serve 4
- 1 lb (700 g) braising steak
- 2 tbsp (15 g) flour • salt
- pepper • 1 large onion
- 1 large carrot • half pint (300 ml) pale ale
- 1 tbsp (15 ml) red wine vinegar • 1 tbsp (15 g) brown sugar • quarter pint (150 ml) beef stock

For the pastry
- 8 oz (225 g) self-raising flour
- salt • 3 oz (75 g) butter
- flour for rolling out the pastry

INDEX

Acknowledgements

The publishers would like to thank all those who have contributed
to the preparation of this book, in particular:

Angie Allison, David Bême, Antoine Caron, Jean-Jacques Carreras,
Aude Desmortiers, Rupert Hasterok, Nicolas Lemaire, Hervé Levano,
Mike Mayor, Kha Luan Pham, Vincent Pompougnac,
Marie-Laure Ungemuth, Emmanuèle Zumstein.

Creative Workshop:
Talya Kahn (p.132-133), Anne Jochum (p. 136-137).

Translation: Lucilla Watson.

Picture credits: British Meat Information Service (p. 140-141).

Illustrations: Franz Rey.

Printed in Italy
Eurolitho – Milan
March 1999